Attitude Motivation

This publication is designed to provide accurate and authoritative information with regard to the subject matter covered. It is sold with the understanding that the publisher is not engaged in rendering legal, accounting, or other professional advice. If legal advice or other professional assistance is required, the services of a competent professional person should be sought.

Written and published by Bob Oros
Copyright. All rights reserved 1992-2012
832 NW 142nd Street
Edmond, OK 73013
405-751-9191
800-480-5197
www.BobOros.com
Bob@BobOros.com

ATTITUDE MOTIVATION	1
THE BEST KEPT SECRET IN THE WORLD!	3
7 SELLING TECHNIQUE AFFIRMATIONS	5
6 SELLING ATTITUDE AFFIRMATIONS	13
90 LEADERSHIP CONCEPTS	20
ATTITUDE TOWARDS SELLING	111
NEGOTIATING PRICE	133
THE SELLING PROCESS	155
ADVANCED TECHNIQUES	177

The best kept secret in the world!

I am going to share with you a secret. Many people don't want you to know this secret because it is so powerful. This secret has been used all through history by kings, presidents, religious leaders, big companies, TV shows, advertisers, politicians, parents, coaches and teachers. It is also used by gang leaders, drug pushers, criminals, bullies, thieves and even the friends you hang out with.

This secret has stood the test of time. In one form or another, this secret been used since the beginning of mankind. Many successful people have used this secret to reach their goals. Many people swear that the discovery of this secret is the single most important event in their lifetime.

Nearly every minute of the day you are being made to do things. How? By the words and pictures you allow people to put in your mind.

The repetition of positive or negative words and pictures day after day begins to affect you, for good or for bad. Your mind begins to make you do the things that the words and pictures represent. The use of this secret is one of the oldest practices of civilization.

The Boy Scout Oath, the Girl Scout oath, the Pledge of Allegiance to the flag, the prayers, quotes and affirmations you are taught are all forms of putting words and images in your mind.

Marketing companies who want you to buy things use words, pictures and TV commercials that make you want to buy things from them. Politicians use words and pictures to make you want to vote for them. Drug pushers use words and pictures to make you buy drugs and get high.

Once these words and pictures are used to make you do certain things, and you continue to do them, you become controlled by your habits. Once the habit becomes stronger and stronger it becomes very difficult to change. Maybe someone can make you do things, and maybe they can't. But one thing is for certain. You will "DO THINGS" and whether you end up a great success, or you end up "average," it will be because of the things YOU MADE YOURSELF DO WITH THE IMAGES AND WORDS YOU USED TO PROGRAM YOUR MIND.

7
Selling Technique Affirmations

1. Planning

To get big results make big plans

I am a perfect example of a well organized sales professional. Every detail of every sales call is planned out well in advance. At any given moment during the day I can look at my schedule, at my list of things-to-do and be right on track. Everything I do is completed step-by-step in perfect order. I spend whatever time it takes to work out the details of every sales call I am going to make during the week. Not simply an itinerary, but everything I want to accomplish with each customer. My customers are always amazed and impressed with the amount of thought and preparation I put into every sales call.

2. Questions

Ask questions that make the sale

I am an expert at asking well thought out questions and I carefully listen to everything my customer says. I have rehearsed the questions that will get the results I am aiming for, which is building a relationship and becoming an important part of my customer's business. I let my customer do most of the talking and they look forward to my visit because I am so interested in them and their business. I keep careful records of the answers and information I get and review them each time I make a repeat call. The customer can almost feel my sincere interest in them.

3. Attention

Get attention with an irresistible offer

Every time I visit a customer I bring them something that will really help their business. It could be a very special price on an item, a piece of industry news, an idea that will help their business, something that will give them a competitive advantage, or perhaps something personal that I knew they were interested in. On every visit my customer says "wow, I really appreciate that!" I never make a call on a customer that is boring or routine. When they see me coming they are sincerely excited to see me because I break the routine of their business by bringing value every time I make a sales call.

4. Presentations

Give reasons why they should buy

My sales calls are so much more than just a visit to get an order. I spend time carefully reviewing the customer's business and meticulously match my products to their problems. I give them a well thought out list of "reasons why" I am the best person to provide the solution to their problem. I have put so much work into preparing my presentation that I can recite it frontwards and backwards. I have studied all the features and benefits of my products as well as everything my company can do to make it easy for the customer to make a well educated decision to buy from me. When it comes to making a presentation there is no one better sold on my company and my products and services than I am.

5. Objections

Remove every roadblock to the sale

I have carefully recorded every objection that a customer has presented to me as a reason why they were not interested in buying. My list has all the objections that I have been presented with from a variety of customers and under numerous conditions. Each one of the objections has been researched and I have carefully crafted a response for each one. Not just a canned response, but a real, sincere, well thought out answer based on facts, experience and product knowledge. I am well aware that 67% of most sales are made after 5 objections and I not only anticipate them, but welcome them as a way for the customer to build confidence in me.

6. Closing

Ask for the order and get paid

I am able to ask for the order in a way that the customer feels good about spending their money with me. I am able to steer the sales process towards a predetermined objective that makes it easy for the customer to go forward and make the commitment. I have done such a good job of presenting my company, my offer and myself that the customer feels no pressure when it comes time to go forward. When I am working with a prospect that may take several visits to bring them all the way through the sales pipeline I have the specific objective clearly defined for each step of the process. I have done such a flawless job of bringing the sale to the point of the close or next step that the process seems smooth and natural.

7. Follow up

Remove all hope for competitors

My follow up is done so well that my customer can count on me to take care of every detail that will make the process of the sale an enjoyable experience. My follow up starts as soon as I make an initial contact over the phone before the actual visit. I send confirmation letters and recap memos before the sale, during the sale and after the sale. Even if I don't get the sale in the time frame I anticipated, I know that it will only be a matter of time, so my follow up continues with weekly or monthly cards or letters. I stay in touch, keep good records of every contact with the customer, and can put my finger in any piece of information I may need whenever it is necessary.

6
Selling Attitude Affirmations

1. Attitude

Define what I want and go after it

Being aggressive means moving towards what I want with the Right Mental Attitude and taking for granted that I will get it. I have a clearly defined objective and I am automatically moving toward it. Any problems or obstacles I encounter are welcomed as opportunities. They will not stop me; they only mean I have to work harder. If I make mistakes I face up to them and correct my course of action. I am never bothered by what anyone says because they do not have all the facts and are speaking on impulse. I never allow myself to be intimidated or taken advantage of. I have a huge amount of knowledge and experience and do not have to take a back seat to anyone. Being aggressive and going after what I want will assure me of developing my sales ability to its full potential.

2. Respect

Earn respect by being an expert

I have earned the respect and trust of my customers by being an expert in my business. I am always on the lookout for new ideas; new information and new products that will help my customers grow their business. I read the trade journals, I study new products, I watch my competition and I am a valuable source of news and information for my customers. I can be trusted with confidential information my customers share with me and I never engage in gossip or criticism about other people or other companies. I never put down my competition or the competition of my customers. Because of this integrity my customer has complete confidence in me and respect for the way I conduct my business.

3. Service

Help customers build their business

My primary goal is to help my customer become more successful. I am not just selling products and services they can buy from any competitor; I am selling them ideas, consulting services and my personal services. I can proudly say that "I" go with every order and I truly make a difference in their business. While my competitors may be looking at the commission they make, I am more concerned with helping my customer make more money and improve their business. My products and services were created to help my customers solve a problem. My customers buy from me because I am able to convey this helpful approach on every sales call and in every meeting with my customers.

4. Urgency

Be enthusiastic get things done now

I have a sense of urgency that is as fast as a bolt of lightening. When I receive an emergency call from a customer I immediately respond with massive action and a whatever-it-takes approach to solve the problem. I return phone calls immediately. My reaction time is measured in minutes not hours or days. If I see a problem coming I call my customer in advance and begin solving the problem before it even begins. My highest priority is serving my customer and I take full responsibility for my actions and the actions of my company. My customer knows they can count on me and they never worry because I am their insurance policy against frustration and unresolved problems.

5. Confidence

Remove restrictions and limitations

I am confident because I have removed the self imposed restrictions and limitations that hold people back from accomplishing all they can. My goal is to become a highly skilled sales professional. I have made a total commitment and it is reflected in every action I take and every task I perform. While my colleagues and competitors are always looking for an easier way to get their job done by reducing the amount of service they give, I am perfecting the skills that will make me a major league player in my own game, the game of selling. My confidence goes deep because I have earned it by attending sales meetings with enthusiasm, investing in time beyond my company training to improve my skills, and setting high goals.

6. Persistence

Keep going and never give up

My persistence comes from being committed to my goals and my willingness to keep going when everyone else would give up. When I am faced with an impossible task it does not stop you, it brings out the best in me. When most people fear changes that have to be made, I see them as opportunities to improve, to learn something new, to develop a new skill. When it comes to landing a new customer I know that it can take time so I begin well in advance so I don't have to scramble around trying to replace a lost customer. I am always looking for new business, calling on new customers, getting referrals and keeping the pipeline full of potential customers. My persistence and steadiness of purpose guarantees my selling success.

90 Leadership Concepts

1

"Campaigns and battles are nothing but a long series of difficulties to be overcome. The lack of equipment, the lack of food, the lack of this or that; the real leader displays his quality in his triumphs over adversity, however great the adversity may be."

General George C. Marshall, US Army

2

"How many things apparently impossible have nevertheless been performed by resolute men who had no alternatives but death!"

Napoleon Bonaparte, French Emperor

3

"I'm a hell of a general when I'm winning, anybody is, but it's when you're not winning – and I have not always been winning… -it is then that the real test of leadership is made."

Field Marshal Sir William Slim, British Army

4

"DIFFICULTIES is the name given to things which it is our business to overcome."

Admiral Ernest J King, US Navy

5

"Do not compare your physical forces with those of the enemy's, for the spirit should not be compared with matter."

General Simon Bolivar, South American Revolutionary

6

"It is better to act quickly and err than to hesitate until the time of action is past."

Major General Carl Von Clausewitz, Prussian Army

7

"Find out where your enemy is. Get at him as soon as you can and as often as you can, and keep moving on."

General Ulysses S Grant, US Army

8

"It is the cold glitter in the attacker's eye not the point of the questing bayonet that breaks the line."

General George S Patton, Jr, US Army

9

"It is fatal to enter any war without the will to win it."

General Douglas MacArthur, US Army

10

"Officers can never act with competence until they are masters of their profession."

Major General Henry Knox, Continental Army

11

"Issuing orders is worth about 10 percent. The remaining 90 percent consists of assuring proper and vigorous execution of the order."

General George S. Patton, Jr, US Army

12

"They won't believe you if you shoot bull. When you face ranks of men and try that, you can hear 'em sigh in despair when you open your mouth, if they sense you're a phony."

Lieutenant General Lewis Puller, US Marine Corps

13

"Don't go and tell men something that you don't believe yourself, because they'll spot it and if they don't spot it at the time, they'll find out. Then you're finished.

Field Marshal Sir William Slim, British Army

14

"Bravery is the capacity to perform properly even when scared half to death."

General Omar Bradley, US Army

15

"The most essential qualities of a general will always be: first, a high moral courage, capable of great resolution; second a physical courage which takes no account of danger. Scientific or military acquirements are secondary to these."

General Henri De Jomini, Russian Army

16

"It doesn't do any good to fake a thing, to fake an ill or a benefit. We have to face the facts the way they are, not the way we wish they were. If we start with a false situation, then we're getting off on the wrong foot to begin with. A clear concise awareness of the exact condition, the exact problem which faces an individual is his best weapon for coping with it."

General Curtis E. LeMay, US Air force

17

"In 40 hours I shall be in battle, with little information, and on the spur of the moment will have to make momentous decisions. But I believe that one's spirit enlarges with responsibility and that with God's help, I shall make them right."

General George S. Patton, Jr, US Army

18

"True decision making, by its nature, in combat and elsewhere consists in determining a line of action when choices are equally difficult."

Brigadier General SLA Marshall, US Army

19

"Nothing is more difficult, and therefore more precious, than to be able to decide."

Napoleon Bonaparte, French Emperor

20

"Bold decisions give the best promise of success."

Field Marshal Erwin Rommel, German Army

21

"A battle is lost less through the loss of men than by discouragement."

Frederick The Great, German Emperor

22

"Of the many harms that can beset an army, vacillation is the greatest. Of the disasters that can befall an army, none surpasses doubt."

General Chiang Shang, Ancient Chinese General

23

"An irresolute general… although at the head of an army superior in number to that of the enemy, finds himself always inferior on the field of battle."

Napoleon Bonaparte, French Emperor

24

"All men are afraid in battle. The coward is the one who lets his fear overcome his sense of duty."

General George S Patton, Jr US Army

25

"Shrewd critics have assigned military success to all manner of things -tactics, shape of frontiers, speed, well placed rivers, mountains or woods, intellectual ability, or the use of artillery. All in a measure true, but non vital. The secret lies in the inspiring spirit which lifted weary, footsore men out of themselves and made them march forgetful of agony."

General George S Patton, Jr, US Army

26

"A lost battle is a battle one thinks one has lost."

Field Marshal Ferdinand Foch, French Army

27

"He who in war fails to do what he undertakes, may always plead the accidents which invariably attend military affairs: but he who declares a thing to be impossible, which is subsequently accomplished, registers his own incapacity."

Field Marshal Arthur Wellesley, British Army

28

"The history of failure in war can be summed up in two words: too late. Too late in comprehending the deadly purpose of a potential enemy; too late in realizing the mortal danger; too late in preparedness; too late in uniting all possible forces for resistance; too late in standing with one's friends."

General Douglas MacArthur, US Army

29

"All men are frightened. The more intelligent they are, the more they are frightened. The courageous man is the man who forces himself, in spite of his fear, to carry on."

General George S Patton, Jr, US Army

30

"Fear unhinges the will, and by unhinging the will it paralyzes the reason; thoughts are dispersed in all directions in place of being concentrated on one definite aim... While moral fear is largely overcome by courage based on reason, physical fear is overcome by courage based on physical action."

Major General JFC Fuller, British Army

31

"Fear is the beginning of wisdom."

General William Sherman, US Army

32

"We must make allowance for delays and difficulties..."

General Robert El Lee, Confederate Army

33

"They made their plans just as you might make a splendid set of harness. It looks good; and answers well; until it gets broken; and then they are done for. I made my plans of ropes. If anything went wrong, I tied a knot; and went on."

Field Marshal Arthur Wesseley, British Army

34

"Every commander must firmly grasp the fact that slavery to routine and extreme enthusiasms for some specific plan or some specific method are the most dangerous thing for all of us... nothing can be absolute or solidly fixed; everything flows and changes, and any means, any methods might be used in a certain situation."

General Mikhail V. Frunze, Soviet Army

35

"Pursue one great decisive aim with force and determination."

Major General Karl Von Clausewitz, Prussian Army

36

"The man who tries to hold on to everything ends up by holding nothing."

Frederick The Great, German Emperor

37

"Many good generals exist in Europe, but they see too many things at once: I see but one thing..."

Napoleon Bonaparte, French Emperor

38

"To preserve a clear and well-defined purpose at every instant of time, and to cause all efforts to converge on that end."

General William T Sherman, US Army

39

"In selecting the proper objective the air leader must consider not alone his capacity and his own desires, but he must consider the mission of the ground forces and the concerted effort and plan of the whole force."

General Henry H Arnold, US Air Force

40

"A leader is a dealer in hope."

Napoleon Bonaparte, Emperor of France

41

"Hope encourages men to endure and attempt everything; in depriving them of it, or in making it too distant, you deprive them of their very soul."

Field Marshal Maurice Comte De Saxe, French Army

42

"The principle task of a general is mental..."

Frederick The Great, German Emperor

43

"The credit belongs to the man who is actually in the arena, whose face is marred by dust and sweat and blood; who strives valiantly; who errs and comes short again and again, who knows the great enthusiasms, the great devotions, and spends himself in a worthy cause; who at best, knows the triumph of high achievement; and who, at the worst, if he fails, at least fails while daring greatly, so that his place shall never be with those cold and timid souls who know neither victory nor defeat."

Theodore Roosevelt

44

"To speak of the importance of a sense of humor would be futile, if it were not that what cramps so many men isn't that they are by nature humorless as they are hesitant to excretes what humor they possess."

Brigadier General SLA Marshall, US Army

45

"Humor is an effective but tricky technique in command and leadership, beneficial when used wisely, but it can backfire into a dangerous boob-trap if overworked or crudely employed."

Major General Perry M. Smith, US Air Force

46

"When things are going badly in battle the best tonic is to take one's mind off one's own troubles by considering what a rotten time one's opponent must be having."

Field Marshal Archibald Wavell, British Army

47

"The most indispensable attribute of the great captain is imagination."

General Douglas MacArthur, US Army

48

"If I always appear prepared, it is because before entering an undertaking, I have meditated for many days and have foreseen what may occur. It is not genius which reveals to me suddenly and secretly what I should do in certain circumstances, it is thought and mediation."

Napoleon Bonaparte, French Emperor

49

"There is no victory except through our imaginations."

General Dwight D Eisenhower, US Army

50

"Originality, not conventionality, is one of the main pillars of generalship."

Major General JFC Fuller, British Army

51

"The impossible can only be overborne by the unprecedented."

General Sir Ian Hamilton, British Army

52

"During war the ball is always kicking around loose in the middle of the field and any man who has the will may pick it up and run with it."

Brigadier General SAL Marshall, US Army

53

"I have never given a damn what the enemy was going to do or where he was. What I have known is what I intended to do and then have done it."

General George S Patton, US Army

54

"I learned that good judgment comes from experience and that experience grows out of mistakes."

General Omar N Bradley, US Army

55

"What you have to do is to weigh all the various factors, recognizing that in war half your information my be wrong, that a lot of it is missing completely, and that there are all sorts of elements over which you have not control... You have got to weigh all these things and come to a decision as to what you want to do."

Field Marshal Sir William Slim, British Army

56

"A man has justice if he acknowledges the interests of all concerned in any particular transaction rather than serving his own particular interests."

General SLA Marshall, US Army

57

"Nothing destroys effectiveness any faster than a lack of integrity or a lack of confidence."

General Ronald R Fogleman, US Air Force

58

"The principles of leadership in the military are the same as they are in business, in the church, and elsewhere:

a. Learn your job (this involves study and hard work). b. Work hard at your job. c. Train your people. d. Inspect frequently to see that the job is being done properly."

Admiral Hyman G Rickover, US Navy

59

"A competent leader can get efficient service from poor troops, while on the contrary an incapable leader can demoralize the best of troops."

General John J. Pershing, US Army

60

"I don't think you have to be wearing stars on your shoulders or have "commander" in your title to be a leader. Anybody who wants to raise his hand can be a leader any time."

General Ronald R Fogleman, US Air Force

61

"War is not an affair of chance. A great deal of knowledge, study, and meditation is necessary to conduct it well."

Frederick The Great, German Emperor

62

"A liberally educated person meets new ideas with curiosity and fascination. An illiberally educated person meets new ideas with fear."

Vice Admiral James B Stockdale, US Navy

63

"Officers, particularly those in positions of command, must at all times be urged to expand the scope of their knowledge; nothing has a more damaging effect on the quality of the army than a hard core of commanders whose minds are narrow and inflexible."

Major General Yigael Allon, Army of Israel

64

"Communications dominate war; broadly considered, they are the most important single element in strategy, political or military."

Rear Admiral Alfred Mahan, US Navy

65

"Luck in the long run is given only to the efficient."

Field Marshal Helmuth Von Molke, German Army

66

"Most army officers who grumble about the luck of their more favored brothers either are not honest with themselves or they have not taken the pains to analyze the reason for the success of their more fortunate fellow officers."

General Henry H Arnold, US Air Force

67

"When a general conducts himself with all prudence, he still can suffer ill fortune; for how many things oppose his labors! Weather, harvest, his officers, the health of his troops, blunders, the death of an officer on whom he counts, discouragement of the troops, exposure of his spies, negligence of the officers who should reconnoiter the enemy and, finally betrayal. These are the things that should be kept continually before your eyes so as to be prepared for them and prevent good fortune from blinding us."

Frederick The Great, German Emperor

68

"I base my calculation on the expectation that luck will be against me."

Napoleon Bonaparte, French Emperor

69

"Fortune or fate decides one half our life; the other half depends on ourselves."

Field Marshal Bernard L Montgomerey, British Army

70

"When a man has committed no faults in war, he can only have been engaged in it but a short time."

Marshal Bicomte De Turene, French Army

71

"The capability of an individual and the capability of a ship can be enhanced by some 20 to 30 percent if morale is high."

Admiral Elmo R Zumwalt, Jr., US Navy

72

"The important thing is to see the opportunity and know how to use it."

Field Marshal Maurice Comte De Saxe, French Army

73

"Optimism and pessimism are infectious and they spread more rapidly from the head downward that in any other direction... I firmly determined that my mannerisms and speech in public would always reflect the cheerful certainty of victory -that any pessimism and discouragement I might ever feel would be reserved for my pillow."

General Dwight D Eisenhower, US Army

74

"A pragmatically optimistic individual who is not a Pollyanna, but who comes to work with a lot of enthusiasm and optimism, tends to be an effective and respected leader. Although a cynic might do a good job as a leader, this cynicism and pessimism may soon transfer negatively throughout the organization."

Major General Perry M Smith, US Air Force

75

"There's your target and this is your axis of advance. Don't signal me during the fighting for more men, arms or vehicles. All that we could allocate you've already got, and there isn't more. Keep signaling your advances."

Lt General Moshe Dayan, Army of Israel

76

"A general's principal talent consists in knowing the mentality of the soldier and in winning his confidence."

Napoleon Bonaparte, French Emperor

77

"There must be a beginning of any great matter, but the continuing unto the end until it be thoroughly finished yields the true glory."

Admiral Sir Francis Drake, British Navy

78

"We fight, get beat, rise, fight again."

Major General Nathaniel Greene, Continental Army

79

"In case of doubt, push on just a little further and then keep on pushing."

General George s Patton, Jr., US Army

80

"One of my superstitions had always been when I started to go anywhere, or do anything, not to turn back, or stop until the thing intended was accomplished."

General Ulysses S Grant, US Army

81

"The advantages of the enemy will have but little value if we do not permit them to impair our resolution."

General Robert E. Lee, Confederate Army

82

"In war nothing is achieved except by calculation. Everything that is not soundly planned in its details yields no result."

Napoleon Bonaparte, French Emperor

83

"A good plan violently executed NOW is better than a perfect plan next week."

General George S Patton Jr, US Army

84

"Since preparedness ensures success and unpreparedness spells failure, there can be no victory in war without advance planning and preparations."

Mao Tse-Tung, Chinese Revolutionary Leader

85

"The best form of "welfare" for the troops is first class training, for this saves unnecessary casualties."

Field Marshal Erwin Rommel, German Army

86

"A sense of humor is part of the art of leadership, of getting along with people, of getting things done."

General Dwight D Eisenhower, US Army

87

"It is better to struggle with a stallion when the problem is how to hold it back, than to urge on a bull which refuses to budge."

Lt General Moshe Dayan, Army of Israel

88

"Of the many attributes necessary for success two are vital -hard work and absolute integrity."

Field Marshal Bernard L Montgomery, British Army

89

"During an operation decisions have usually to be made at once; there may be no time to review the situation or even to think it through... If the mind is to emerge unscathed from this relentless struggle with the unforeseen, two qualities are indispensable; first, an intellect that, even in the darkest hour, retains some glimmerings of the inner light which leads to truth; and second, the courage to follow this faint light wherever it may lead."

Major General Karl Von Clasewitz, Prussion Army

90

"Morale is the state of mind. It is the steadfastness and courage and hope. It is confidence and zeal and loyalty. It is staying power, the spirit which endures to the end - the will to win. With it all things are possible, without it everything else, planning, preparation, production count for naught."

General George C Marshal, US Army

Attitude towards selling

1

To manage your attitude you must monitor your thoughts and feelings under every selling situation. Approach it as if you were doing a scientific study. When you find that you are reacting negatively to a specific situation, you have found an opportunity to sharpen your skill.

2

Your single goal is to exceed your sales plan. Stop now. Make a list of the BENEFITS you will enjoy by exceeding your sales plan. List all the BENEFITS you will receive once you exceed this goal.

3

Once you start to DO the things necessary for success you will find that you have what it takes. You will then have experience. You will then have specific information to work on.

4

Set a 90 day goal. Work towards it every day. Don't look beyond 90 days - just focus on each step it will take to reach your 90 day objective. After you reach it - set another 90 day goal. Once you repeat the process 12 times you will be there.

5

A problem is a chance for you to show your best. We all have problems. Office politics. Perceived defects in the product or service. Impossibly tough competition. Endless personal problems. Unfair commission schedules.

6

The person who continuously looks for new ideas and better methods of selling is the one who moves forward. The person who learns something new, applies it and reapplies it over and over until it becomes a skill.

7

If you say "You get me," you have a good opportunity to prove it. Building credibility during the sales process can make or break the sale – many times it is what the decision is based on.

8

You have to separate yourself from the competition. You have to be different. You have to be better. If you really know what you are talking about, the customer feels it and starts trusting what you say.

9

When someone has the tools to help you succeed and their main purpose is to provide those tools for your use and help you achieve your goals, it is impossible not to feel the desire to work with them.

10

Give your customers the attention and appreciation they are hungry for. Give your prospects the attention and appreciation they are not getting from their current supplier and you will take away the business.

11

Find out by careful listening and questioning what your customer wants and let them know that you are sincerely interested in helping them get it.

12

Most people spend 98% of their time thinking about themselves. In the 2% of time left over there is not much room to squeeze you in.

13

Salespeople frequently make the mistake of offering discounts up front in order to head off a potentially negative discussion about price.

14

Your job is not to talk, but to listen - not to present, but to ask questions.

15

A five year sales goal is much more attainable if it is worked on 90-days at a time. Set your long range goals – but break them down into 90-day increments.

16

To gain the respect of your customers and earn their business, product knowledge should be a daily activity.

17

By adopting an attitude of "do it now" you can solve many small problems before they turn into a lost sale or a lost customer.

18

You have to hit them with a HUGE BENEFIT. A benefit that will have the same power as if you hit them between the eyes with a baseball bat!

19

The bottom line - you get what you expect. Nothing more - nothing less. If you want to increase your sales you have to really EXPECT IT TO HAPPEN. There is only ONE THING that builds expectations – action – doing something productive.

20

To succeed there has to be certain things in harmony. Your expectations and your goals must be equal. If your goals are too high or unrealistic you won't expect to reach them and you will see to it that you get what you expect.

21

Successful sales people make plenty of mistakes; however they relive and build on their achievements and successes resulting in higher and higher expectations.

Negotiating Price

22

If you give a discount too easily or too quickly you have actually cheated the customer out of the feeling that he or she made a good purchase.

23

Your goal is to weave the facts into the conversation that makes the buyer understand the LIGITIMACY of what you are saying.

24

Be shocked at their price shock. This is designed to neutralize the strategy. The customer is shocked at your price; you are shocked at their shock.

25

When making YOUR presentation it is to your advantage to present a higher authority from which you must get approval.

26

Good guy/bad guy occurs when there are two or more buyers and one is easier to get along with, provides more information, or seems more anxious to make a deal, while the other is more difficult.

27

What should you do when someone asks you if that is the best you can do? Simply say yes.

28

Abraham Lincoln would never argue or attack an opponent. In fact, Lincoln, at first, would argue his opponent's case telling all the reasons why his opponent was right. He'd appear to agree to all the things his opponent said.

29

You will get better answers if you are slow to understand. The trouble is that most of us want to look good. We find it hard to say, "I don't know" or "tell me that again."

30

Don't be shy when you state your original price - put on a show of confidence. Amateurs almost always hesitate when giving their first price and professionals very seldom do.

31

If everyone is always beating you up on price, maybe it is because of the way you are presenting it. Presenting your price with implied flexibility should be used as a tool, not as the normal way you present it.

32

Once you make a decision your mind does a search, similar to a computer doing a search for additional information. Your mind is looking for ways to justify the decision you just made.

33

If customers are not loyal, perhaps it is because when you give everything you have, you do not ask for anything in return. Trading builds a relationship.

34

Buyers sometimes use the bait and switch by asking for a price on a large quantity and then order a smaller quantity trying to get you to agree to your first price.

35

The person who offers to split the difference has essentially revealed what they will settle for. You, a seller, should always let the buyer be the one to offer to split the difference first.

36

We find out what everybody else is doing and what everybody else thinks – and conclude that they must be right – and make the decision that I am going to do the same thing.

37

Before you go in to see the customer carefully list five things you want to discuss. When you are in the buyers office, place this list where the buyer can easily see it.

38

You don't sell your products to some huge organization that makes rational decisions based on logical data and facts. You sell to a human, emotional, somewhat irrational person who makes the decision based on issues of ego, personality and irrationality.

39

The next time you are faced with a really tough customer, one that always gives you a hard time about everything, try this: Ask for their advice on something.

40

Ask your customers what they are willing to pay more for. The answer will tell you how you can justify your prices rather than discount them.

41

To overcome resistance the best approach is to gather sufficient information about the buyer as well as the products or ideas you are going to present.

42

The next time you present a product to a customer take two products instead of one. Take in an overpriced high end product along with the one you want to sell. Show them the over priced, high end product first. After they get over their shock, bring out the one you wanted to sell in the first place and it will seem like an easy choice.

The Selling Process

43

The bottom line of planning; spend at least four hours on a Friday afternoon or Saturday morning going through each call you are going to make next week.

44

Asking questions rather than talking and making positive statements puts us in the category of a consultant. The true purpose of a consultative sales person is to find out what your customer wants and help them get it.

45

Every time we call on one of our accounts to present a new product or service, or even to simply get an order, there is a preliminary process we must go through or we will lose before we even begin. We must have their full attention.

46

Ninety percent of the excitement in the present is the imaginary picture we are constantly recreating in our minds of a tomorrow.

47

Always keep in mind that the buyer is comfortable dealing with the sales person and company they are buying from. To make a change requires assurances that you will be able to handle their business.

48

Always know what you want before making the call, and then do what only one in four sales people do; never be shy about asking for it.

49

The satisfaction that comes from doing one thing absolutely right and putting the trade-mark of your character on it, far outweighs the value of a thousand half done jobs.

50

The first step in marketing is to identify your target customer and determine how many customers it will take to maintain your business.

51

Never knock the competitors. But do make sure that your customer knows the difference and appreciates what it will mean if your product is bought.

52

An important thing to remember is that you cannot really sell anybody anything - you can only help them make a good decision. To get a price higher than your competitor you have to list all the reasons they should decide to buy from you.

53

Price is a vitally important element in your market strategy. You can usually change it quickly, unlike your product or its packaging.

54

A professional sales person will spend at least one hour in planning time for each day of selling. It takes that much time to write letters, make appointments, prepare presentations and carefully think about the details of each call you are going to make.

55

Follow-up is something you can control. A daily to-do system, writing everything down in one place, carrying out your promises, returning all customer calls within two to three hours, checking voice mail every two or three hours and updating your message, sending follow up letters, notifying customers of bad news, delays and coming up with alternatives. All these things are under your direct control.

56

If you have a really good reason why your customers should buy from you, and let them know about it on every call, your professional image will go up.

57

As a sales person there are several things you can do on the personal level that will make you unique. The first thing you can do is show up.

58

Selling any type of products without an organized plan will produce only average or below average results. Every plan starts with a specific daily objective - a list: What are the things I have to do today?

59

Confidence simply means knowing how something will turn out before it happens. Visualize the end results and your confidence will go up.

60

With the right attitude towards everyone you come in contact with you can stop being your own worst enemy and have them respond favorably to you.

61

You must have an opener which breaks through their attitude and provoke the prospect to say, "Sure, I'll listen to what you have to say with an open mind. Come on in and tell your story."

62

The mental picture you have of your customer before you walk through the door will greatly affect the response you get.

63

Never hesitate to ask about their family if there is a picture, their golf score if there is a trophy, their hunting adventures, favorite fishing spots, backpacking experience, etc.

Advanced techniques

64

Make a habit of calling your customer's attention to new merchandise, to specials, to other items in connection with what they are already buying and you will be enhancing your relationship while increasing your business.

65

When you are talking with a prospect and you have made the call on them, imply that you are only there to see if they qualify for you to spend time and energy helping them solve their problems.

66

Politicians never like to talk about the past and very rarely address issues in the present, it's always the future. "I am your bridge to the 21st century". "Your door to the future."

67

Put your customers on the "magic carpet" and take them to a place where their future becomes a possible reality. You won't have to sell, you will only have to help them buy!

68

Organize your presentation in a way that will make the best appeal to his or her buying senses ... sight, hearing and touch.

69

The finest check you can use to avoid making the common mistake of becoming too technical is to keep in mind constantly your objective, to build a picture of the prospect - seeing him or her using your product.

70

If you have been successful in transporting the person in front of you to a state of incompleteness where he or she sees themselves using what you are selling, they will do the closing.

71

When answering "smoke screen" objections the normal response is to agree with the objection, however, the best response is to say "I'm glad you brought that up!" And then ask a question.

72

No matter how hard you worked or how many concessions you have made when you sell a customer, he or she still feels that you owe them a favor.

73

Harvard University released a report recently that said recognition is the most powerful motivator!

74

Working without a schedule, making unprepared calls, spending too much time on marginal or unprofitable accounts, taking too many small orders and not making good use of the telephone are just a few of the old habits that do not work any more.

75

Assume the customer or prospect has not really raised an objection but that he or she has asked for information.

76

To answer an objection by denying it is rarely good practice. A denial is justified, however, If the objection is obviously untrue.

77

You might be tempted to lower your price, instead, call their bluff. "Okay, here's what I can do. Find the best price you can and I'll beat it by at least 10 percent! But I get to choose when we deliver." "I get to select the quality that we ship."

78

You know the value of intelligent, dramatic, forceful, suggestive closing when you feel in your heart you are rendering a great service by helping the buyer to decide something for the buyer's own good.

79

The compelling attitude of unshakable CONFIDENCE on your part when closing is the result of a feeling in your heart that what you have will benefit the customer.

80

Don't be timid about ASKING FOR THE ORDER. He or she expects you to; he or she knows you are not a "greeter" but a person hired to sell.

81

If you are dealing with a person who is not afraid to ask for what they want and you have only a vague idea of what you want, it is like going into a gun fight with no bullets in your gun.

82

There is no faster way to exceed your sales plan than to aggressively go after new accounts.

83

If you don't call on the customer and ask for the order, the sale is lost anyway. If you call on him or her and flop, you will not be any worse off than you are right now, so you have nothing to lose. When you strike out a few times you get over the fear of failure.

84

When buying products, customers don't generalize, they think in specifics. The next time you introduce a new product to your accounts, focus on the specifics.

www.ingramcontent.com/pod-product-compliance
Lightning Source LLC
Chambersburg PA
CBHW032004170526
45157CB00002B/535